SUNBUDDY
FABLES

BOOK 6

ALSO BY RAE DORNAN:

Available in paperback, kindle and audio:
Freddie's Ayurvedic Adventure
The Weekend Retreat
British Justice Me Lud
Sunbuddy Fables #1-10
SunRae Healing Book

Available in audio only:
African Storybook
Rae's Rhythms

SUNBUDDY
FABLES

BOOK 6

Copyright © 2014 Rae Dornan
www.SunRaeProductions.com

All rights reserved.
For permission to reproduce parts of this book, please contact the author.

Cover and book design by Andrew Osta
www.AndrewOsta.com

First Printing: USA, July 2014
ISBN 978-0-9896218-8-5

THE TWO
GREEDY SQUIRRELS

(London UK) 15-06-1995

THE TWO GREEDY SQUIRRELS

1.

Two squirrels lived
in a London park,

Bickering constantly,
from dawn till dark.

Their battle began
on a cloudy day,

When one thought
the other was away.

2.

Lots happening,
full-on activity,

Birds giving it plenty,
on every tree.

Singing their best,
to prove their worth,

To continue their bloodline,
giving birth.

3.

Priorities differed,
in this period of time,

As ducks waddled
through pond slime.

Different energy levels,
extended out

All frantically raced
and flew about.

4.

Trees blossomed,
buds had their time,

Life was abundant,
in the summer clime.

The packed scene,
had honest endeavour,

As squirrels gathered
for the cold weather.

5.

They're busy creatures
and very wary,

Avoiding humans,
who they find scary.

This changes
when squirrels steal food,

Becoming aggressive,
in a foul mood.

6.

Two males,
wanted every acorn around,

From others,
or those fallen to the ground.

One decided to steal
another's stash,

But was spotted
and received a bash.

7.

The other said,
"Take some of that!"

He saw stars that appeared,
just like that.

Stars he liked
but not inside his brain

As they always came
with lots of pain.

8.

He ran off
as fast as his legs would scurry,

Hotly pursued by the other
in a hurry.

Who was livid,
in shock and disbelief,

Furiously chasing,
the furry tailed thief.

9.

He'd have done
exactly the same,

Robbing the other
feeling no shame.

The chase was on
around the tree,

The thieving squirrel,
tried to flee.

10.

They nearly broke,
the four minute mile,

Spectacularly moving,
with grace and guile.

Higher and higher
every second in time,

Their claws dug deep,
on the climb.

11.

Finally the guilty one
had nowhere to flee,

He leapt on the branch,
of another tree.

This daring manoeuvre,
nearly won the day,

But the wronged one,
also leapt into the fray.

12.

Birds squawked,
leaves fell on the ground,

Created from,
the scurrying around.

The embattled tree
was excessively clawed,

Both were exhausted,
respect restored.

13.

Both retired,
to their acorn stash,

Figuring what happened,
in a flash.

They'd been robbed,
so unfair!

As both stared,
at lots of thin air.

14.

An opportunist squirrel,
had seen it all,

As both raced up,
the oak tree so tall.

Wagging his tail,
he robbed them blind,

For him,
this was a wonderful find.

15.

It was all too much,
for the fluffy two,

Nothing learnt,
they didn't have a clue.

Frantically gathering acorns,
big and small,

So they'd have a stash
for the coming fall.

16.

No one said,
a squirrel's life was fair,

They don't live
by an equal share.

The opportunist,
did he keep his stash?

He was robbed the next day,
quick as a flash!

DON THE DRAGONFLY

(Florida, USA) 16-06-1995

DON THE DRAGONFLY

1.

Don was
as skilful as could be

Manoeuvring,
around every tree.

He was able to do
many things,

Reason was
he had four wings.

2.

He'd hover,
or fly high in the sky,

It was easy,
he just had to try.

Flying left,
or zooming right,

He really was
an amazing sight.

3.

He constantly wondered,
about what to do

Confused of late,
he didn't have a clue.

Things went wrong,
and this is how it started,

When he took his wonderful gifts
for granted.

4.

He lived in a climate,
balmy and warm,

As things settled down,
after a storm.

The air was crisp,
heat rose from the ground,

Nature was on the move,
activity all around.

DON THE DRAGONFLY

5.

Don said, "Big deal,
it's all been done before.

Nothing's new after a storm,
this I'm sure.

Others think I'm amazing,
with huge eyes.

I'm not the only one,
look at flies!"

6.

He hovered about
totally depressed,

Not feeling unique,
not heaven blessed.

"Nothing new,
ever happens to me!

I might as well,
been born a flea."

7.

This attitude continued
for quite a while,

Other dragonflies left,
as he'd forgotten to smile.

Don said, "They'll be
other creatures, I'll find.

New Age nonsense bores me,
always being kind."

8.

While he was whining
and acting absurd,

He was being observed
by a predatory bird.

The hungry bird didn't care
how he did feel,

Thinking, "Dinner is that
four winged meal."

9.

He plunged head first,
at a frightening speed,

His stomach grumbled,
due to a pressing need.

At the last second,
Don sensed danger up on high,

And flew sideways,
across the clear blue sky.

10.

He deflected,
the two winged assassin's beak,

But was stunned,
immediately going weak.

Plummeting downwards,
at an alarming rate,

The bird turned towards him,
to seal his fate.

11.

Don's boredom had left
in a hurry,

As his life
had a new instant worry.

He hoped to survive,
to see the sunrise,

From a bird who felt nothing,
for his demise.

12.

Don knew
he was coming his way,

He used his ability
to live another day.

Shimming left,
he instantly took off right,

Blown sideways,
as the bird passed in flight.

DON THE DRAGONFLY

13.

The bird gave up,
and went elsewhere

To find another dish,
which he wouldn't share.

Don went to a reed,
to recover and rest,

This had been
an enormous test.

14.

Everything seemed
more vibrant and clear,

He visibly relaxed
from his fear.

Apathy for life
was totally blown,

He never took for granted
his green home.

15.

He realized
how lucky he'd been

He could easily be in a stomach,
never again seen.

He marvelled at
having four wonderful wings,

Knowing now
they were heaven sent things.

DAVE THE DUCK

(London UK) 16-06-1995

DAVE THE DUCK

1.

Dave had two wonderful
webbed feet,

Attached to his legs,
making him complete.

Swimming around,
as graceful as could be

Poetry in motion
as he'd glide past a tree.

2.

On the pond's surface,
he never broke stride.

His webbed feet,
gave him immense pride.

Kicking harder,
he'd easily double his pace,

You'd have no chance,
in a paddling race.

3.

At times he acted
like a bighead,

But in nature,
one slip and your dead!

It was a game of dare
he used to play,

Why he did it,
only be could say.

4.

He'd run wildly,
on the dry land,

Thinking he looked
ever so grand.

He tried to impress
all were included,

On occasions,
he was sadly deluded.

5.

Quacking,
"I'm not scared of any at all!

Any dogs,
or their masters so tall."

He was a spectacle,
for all to see,

But was heading
for a catastrophe.

6.

A Golden Retriever,
saw him strut his stuff,

This being his territory,
he'd seen enough.

Ducks are better,
than any bird or mole,

Thinking,
"He's dinner, for my bowl."

7.

Creeping up,
his nose pointing the way,

No joke now,
He wasn't here to play.

Dog wanted
to kill that strutting duck,

Dave the duck
was now out of luck.

8.

Oblivious to
the aggressive vibrations,

Time drew near,
to meet dead relations.

His quacking
disturbed the silent air,

As he gave it plenty,
without a care.

DAVE THE DUCK

9.

Dog attacked,
bowling Dave into the water,

On him in a flash,
giving him no quarter.

The retriever dived in
job almost done,

Close to his prey,
he'd rightfully won.

10.

Dave couldn't fly,
since his fall,

Trying to retreat
by any means at all.

His fab' feet,
came into their glory,

An important part
of this story.

11.

He swam away,
using both webbed feet,

Avoiding dog's mouth,
and obvious defeat.

Canine did
a mean doggie paddle stroke,

Dave gave it his all,
going for broke.

12.

Fear's wonderful,
to make you move fast,

When life depends
on not finishing last.

Dave used all his energy,
all at once,

He'd been stupid,
but wasn't a dunce.

13.

Dog was furious,
that duck got away,

He'd ruined
the retriever's day.

He learnt about
not trying to be funny,

As you'll end up,
as a dead dummy.

14.

No need to show off
or compete,

Or be too big,
for your webbed feet.

Dave's alive,
and is a fortunate duck,

Due to webbed feet,
and plenty of luck.

IAN THE INSECT

(London, UK) 08-06-1995

IAN THE INSECT

1.

Ian's shape
was totally unique,

Looking weird,
even at his peak.

Having twelve legs,
he didn't care

He knew
he'd got his fair share.

2.

Others laughed,
about things of his head,

With comments like,
"I'd rather be dead!"

He had two antennae,
attached to a skull,

Guaranteeing that
he never looked dull.

3.

Bigger than his legs,
in the final shout

In proportion to his body,
huge to carry about.

Scanning in front,
for food or danger,

Not wanting to be eaten
by any stranger.

4.

His armoured shell
resembled an armadillo,

Why he was made like this,
none did know.

A brown shell with black stripes,
gave off a sheen,

It would melt the heart
of any princess or queen.

IAN THE INSECT

5.

He was beautiful,
as he was meant to be

Passive too,
never disturbing an ant or flea.

He was mocked,
because of his antennas,

He was ridiculed,
in all sorts of weathers.

6.

A kindly soul,
just getting on with his life,

A low life form already,
needing no strife.

He dutifully got on
with his daily load,

Happy being an insect,
and not a toad.

7.

Ian's was in England,
on a hot summer's day,

Minding his business,
he didn't want to play.

Looking for a partner,
to produce young,

He never used
any smooth talking tongue.

8.

Walking along,
with his house on his back,

He stopped abruptly,
sensing a coming attack.

If he continued,
he'd be in ultimate strife,

For insects,
this meant losing your life.

IAN THE INSECT

9.

A spider thought,
he was on a winner,

Fully expecting,
a gourmet dinner.

Ian ran,
as fast as his legs would go,

Being the main dish,
on the menu on show.

10.

Other insects saw,
how he got it right,

All insects scapper,
in a one way fight.

They gave respect,
to his brown armoured case,

He'd gone up in their estimation,
gaining face.

11.

Ian thought,
"My antennae saved the day!

As I'm blind,
they keep danger away."

He always knew
they were just great

Protecting him,
while he looked for a mate.

12.

Who'd seen Ian and thought,
"He looks nifty.

I'd fancy him,
even if he lived to fifty."

This never happen to species
of their kind,

But you take the point,
he was a major find.

IAN THE INSECT

13.

Dangling her proboscis,
next to his own,

Ian was being
well and truly shown.

For insects,
this was love at first sight,

Perfect for each other,
it was just right.

14.

Both strolled,
towards the setting sun,

Hearts in anticipation
as both had won.

Others might think,
they're ugly and sad,

But the offspring,
delighted mum and dad.

SUNBUDDY FABLES #6

15.

Beauty is in
the eyes of the beholders,

Even if they've got antennae,
and no shoulders.

There's reasons,
why creatures are like this

And them being them,
It's absolute bliss.

MEL THE MANATEE

(Florida, USA) 18-05-1995

MEL THE MANATEE

1.

Mel was a lump,
in anyone's book,

All you had to do
was look.

He was big,
passive and meek,

Making his future,
dangerous and bleak.

2.

Two front flippers,
directed him along,

With a massive tail,
he was so strong.

Never shoving his weight,
like a fool,

He wouldn't do that
as he was cool.

SUNBUDDY FABLES #6

3.

Cruising the seas,
at a leisurely pace,

Having no aggression
on his face.

His elephant ancestors,
all agree,

"Dieting," they'd say,
"not for me!"

4.

Like a walrus,
a wonderful sight,

A high life form,
never in a fight.

He had two,
wonderful little eyes,

Never disturbed,
by bugs or flies.

MEL THE MANATEE

5.

Living off an island in Florida,
called Sanibel,

Not knowing danger,
not for him to foretell...

Of the jeopardy from man,
a terrible shame,

As speed boats play,
their recreational game.

6.

The scene was set,
on this particular day,

As the three manatees,
cruised the bay.

All had eaten,
the vegetarians were full up,

Their young not suckling,
no longer a pup.

7.

Constantly surfacing,
the water for air,

Filling their huge lungs,
needing their share.

It's where problems arose,
for passive Mel,

As he's a mammal,
not a coral or shell.

8.

A motor boat skimmed,
over the ocean blue,

The wind was up the sun out
as he nearly flew.

This replenished his soul,
and rid him of strife,

A kindly man,
he loved the sea and natural life.

9.

He felt a thud,
and heard a scream,

Slashed by the boat
this was no dream.

The prop injured Mel,
cutting deep and true,

Red blood poured everywhere
into the blue.

10.

The man knew
this was the case,

Heading for shore,
like in a race.

He went to
a professional vet for help,

Who used cures,
including seaweed and kelp.

11.

He described the disaster,
precise and clear,

The vet assembled,
his equipment and gear.

A commited team,
went towards Mel's pain

It was action stations,
not a time for blame.

12.

Wallowing in blood,
panting and heaving,

He hung by a thread,
barely breathing.

They secured him,
and returned at a rate,

Whether he'd survive
was in the hands of fate.

13.

Every second counted,
that they tried to gain

Attending to the wound,
blood loss, and pain.

With swift treatment,
the blood did stop,

Leaving a scar,
from the motor's prop.

14.

Mel returned,
where loved ones pined for him,

Joyful when he arrived,
in a leisurely swim.

All were reunited,
wonderful for sure,

As his injury,
nearly closed his life's door.

15.

Thanks to committed people,
and what they do

Attending the injured,
who swim the deep blue.

Man will not stop,
in pursuit of joy and pleasure,

Enjoying himself at sea,
whatever the weather.

16.

Spare a thought,
we're in a partnership with others,

Whether it be egrets,
pelicans, or manatee mothers.

We should protect
the magnificent manatee,

Giving hope for another mammal…
Humanity!

ANTON THE ANT

(London, UK) 17-07-1995

ANTON THE ANT

1.

Anton the powerhouse
was everywhere

Surfacing on land,
to deliver his share.

Staying underground,
for the greater good,

He now scaled upwards,
on a piece of wood.

2.

He surfaced with senses,
completely blown,

Because he landed,
on solid 'York Stone.'

He'd ended up,
on a patio in a backyard,

Onto a material,
which was very hard.

3.

He was confused,
as any ant would be

Huge slabs
aren't what you expect to see.

One expects grass,
on the earth's surface,

So ants could get on
with their purpose.

4.

They're insects,
with panache and drive,

Helping their species
to survive.

He thrust out his antennae,
and best feet first,

Entering mother Earth,
with a lightening burst.

5.

Fearlessly marching
towards the unknown,

Amazing,
never being taught or shown.

Courageously continuing,
using no stealth,

Fearless of any danger,
to his health.

6.

"Can't stop,
I got to check this out

Then report back,
on what it's about."

He bumped into a blade of grass,
growing from a crack,

Warily walking around it,
before deciding not to attack.

7.

"Lucky for you,
as I know plenty of soldier ants,

If you'd wear em,
you'd be scared out your pants."

He addressed the grass,
blowing silently in the breeze,

As above his head,
he heard buzzing bees.

8.

He accepted that
the grass was no threat

It wasn't aggressive,
since they'd met.

Briskly moving on,
he stopped in front of a boulder,

Circling the stone,
he pushed it with his shoulder.

ANTON THE ANT

9.

It didn't move,
sensing it wasn't alive or smart,

He reasoned,
"It's got no heat or beating heart."

Moving around the rock,
he gave it a final once over,

Before looking for green grass,
surrounded by clover?

10.

The day had been great,
with so much to do

Different sights, sounds,
and smells all new.

Continually adjusting
to his open air surrounding,

So alive,
his little heart never stopped pounding.

11.

The day waned,
he returned below,

Nature had been
a wonderful show.

Ants adapt,
to whatever situation they find,

Attacking creatures,
deaf, dumb or blind.

12.

Settling down,
he'd done his best,

To keep ants on top,
with countless zest.

He was part
of a ticket called win

"We eat anything,
from any old bin."

13.

"It's my job,
to keep the earth clean,

I was born cruel,
ruthless and mean."

If I was a cow,
I'd want too eat grass,

I'm no vegetarian,
it would be a farce."

14.

"Although I'm explaining
how I feel,

If you fall,
you'll be my next meal.

Imagine how many ants,
you'll be feeding!

I hope you're dead,
as I can't take screaming."

15.

"Just keep moving,
and stay upright,

Sunbathe too long,
I'll give you a bite.

I'm not threatening,
I'm explaining what will be.

I check out the living,
it's my job, you see."

16.

"If you catch me
marauding on the earth's floor,

I'll be checking
that everything's secure.

If it's not,
I'll be telling many a mate,

As feeding my kind,
will be your grisly fate.

17.

"I'm invincible,
let me try and explain.

Ants are the boss
of every domain.

We are minute,
but one of earth's wonders,

Working together
in ridiculous numbers."

WALLY THE (DARTFORD) WARBLER

(Swanage, UK) 04-08-1999

WALLY THE WARBLER

1.

Wally lived happily,
on the Isle of Purbeck,

His kind lived there
longer than any sea wreck.

A secluded nest
was next to bushes of gauze,

He created this perfection
without a pause.

2.

Dartford Warblers
stay all year,

Experts ponder,
the reason's not clear.

But this is where
Wally's found,

Other warblers migrate,
to other ground.

3.

His kind
are very rare,

It's not about
what's right or fair.

Maybe it's
the passage of time,

One reason
is the cold winter clime.

4.

His story begins
on a beautiful Dorset day,

Trying to be invisible,
round Studland Bay.

"It's good the way,
I'm left juicy bugs.

I love all those,
fat slimy slugs?"

5.

"Tourists do their thing,
getting about.

We live together
in the final shout.

Living close to nature
is no crime.

It's how they spend
leisure time,"

6.

"There's few here,
when it's cold.

This is when,
I get bold.

But icy winds
blow in my nest.

Life's very precarious,
at best,"

SUNBUDDY FABLES #6

7.

"I'm staying
in this wonderful habituate,

In summer months,
I get cuddly and fat.

I could live
in southern France or Spain,"

But I'll be here,
though winter's a pain."

8.

"This land I live in
I really love.

Same for
the lark and the dove.

We're not being
a 'Fair Weather Friend,'

As into the environment,
we all blend."

9.

"My ancestors left
for a better life,

But ended up,
with lots of strife.

Warmer climes
werenot a life of bliss,

The greener grass
is what they missed."

10.

"People are accused
for problems on Earth,

But it hasn't affected
my self worth.

This is what
I believe is true,

I don't blame tourists,
or even you."

11.

"Mother Nature's
the likely killer of my kind.

For dartford warblers,
it's tough and a bind.

Only the strong survive,
life on our planet,

Whether human
or the scavenging gannet."

12.

"Protected by bylaws,
or a caring vet.

We all need
any help we can get.

Our existence depends
on lots of luck,

All struggle,
including the common duck."

13.

"Humans don't shorten
our Earth time,

Helping us
is not committing a crime.

Whether we live,
only time will tell.

Maybe it's not to be
our final bell."

14.

"I'll be flying and diving,
calling 'Jer-Jit'

Before returning to my nest,
to snugly fit.

I'll give my all,
do my best not to fail.

You just might see
my white edged tail."

15.

"So thanks for keeping
our habituate together

Protecting me
in the seasons of weather.

But I'll try to hide,
if I know your around,

Born shy,
I'm almost impossible to be found."

16.

He departed in thick undergrowth,
out of sight,

Quickly disappearing,
after his flight.

He's made his home,
in a surprising place,

Having no reason
to condemn the human race.

MEL THE MANATEE'S (Irate) MATE

(London, UK) 07-09-1999

MEL THE MANATEE'S MATE

1.

Mel was as content
as could be,

As he still swam,
in the sea.

He loved his young one
and female mate,

Surviving an accident,
and a gruesome fate.

2.

Living close to humans,
other mammals too,

Many were strange,
not having a clue

About a partnership,
with the sea and earth,

Which they took for granted,
since birth.

3.

This tale is about
another manatee,

Who was not passive,
roaming the sea.

Like a rouge elephant
is close to the truth,

Related to them,
their size is the proof.

4.

Motor boats constantly
flew across the bay,

Slashing manatees,
feeling entitled to play.

He said, "They assume,
speed equates to might,

Reasoning they look
a wonderful sight."

MEL THE MANATEE'S MATE

5.

"They're as bad
as any harpoon,

Taking whales' lives
far to soon.

With my bulk,
small boats I'll attack,

Capsizing them,
from a sideways whack."

6.

He kicked his back flipper,
away from shore,

Going to deeper waters,
from the ocean floor.

He knew humans fishing,
left there boats still,

"That's my destination,
where I'll attack and kill."

7.

Effortlessly cruising,
surfacing for fresh air,

He had bad intentions,
but didn't care.

It was time to show
who was the boss,

By inflicting suffering
on any he came across.

8.

"For millions of years,
we've evolved our species.

In fifty years,
our future lies in pieces.

I'll be hunted,
with my actions considered a sin.

But I'm making a stand,
even though I can't win.

MEL THE MANATEE'S MATE

9.

He saw a shadow,
from a small boat ahead,

Heading straight for it,
his anger fully fed.

Ramming the tiny vessel,
they didn't have a clue,

Screaming on impact,
as bodies hit the deep blue.

10.

Mel felt vibrations of fear
ripple across the sea,

Feeling distress,
even though he couldn't see.

He knew that time
was rapidly running out

As sharks feel fear,
from any distress about.

11.

He pleaded with the other,
full of anger and pride,

Conveying how a boat person
saved his hide.

He touched the other's
higher self,

Touching his soul,
rich and full of wealth.

12.

His anger died,
seeing the only way was to give,

Living in harmony with others,
the way to live.

Both froze,
as they saw a terrifying sight,

Coming towards them
was a 'Great White.'

13.

There are none
that couldn't be slain

A huge shark
is the master of this domain.

Screaming people,
what a scene,

A red sea soon,
opposite of clean.

14.

Manatees swam towards the shark,
so brave,

Knowing help was coming,
as they tried to save...

Those in the water,
which other boats headed for

As others were fishing,
away from the sea shore.

15.

Shark was stunned,
by oncoming manatees

Thinking,
"Have they lost their sanity?"

He swerved,
as help arrived in time,

Departing,
like he'd committed a crime.

16.

People on board,
cried with relief,

Conveying how
they nearly came to grief.

The manatee's mind
was in momentary strife,

But he had saved them,
by risking his life.

THE JUSTICE
OF REGGIE THE RHINO

(London, UK) 11-09-1995

REGGIE THE RHINO

1.

Reggie was happy
with his lot,

As he thought
he'd certainly be shot.

Previously stunned
by a tranquillising dart,

This gave him
a brand new start.

2.

Life was calm,
as he roamed around,

Not afraid
of any new sound.

The Kruger Park is huge,
with no strife,

He hoped to live
with a trouble free life.

3.

Wardens try
to protect wild life there,

All animals
are allowed a fair share.

It's a gift,
for great and small,

For flying birds,
or giraffes so tall.

4.

Humans for once
were no threat

But park animals had a problem,
so all met.

To discuss about
an intolerable situation

Debating the facts,
under consideration.

5.

The spokesanimal was
the pel's fishing owl,

Addressing all,
including the guinea-fowl.

"An elephant
is shoving his weight around,

Bullying all,
a solution has to be found."

6.

"Strutting about,
he's bigger than the rest,

Doing it everywhere
with vigour and zest.

All are opposed,
as he's out of tune,

He destroys trees,
the home of the baboon!"

SUNBUDDY FABLES #6

7.

Reggie knew this,
but wasn't big enough,

The bull was massive,
with too much stuff.

He told the wise owl
he didn't have a clue,

As there wasn't much
he could do.

8.

Later he saw a reflection
in the drinking water,

Of a rhino as broad as him,
who was no shorter.

Reggie approached,
in a passive way,

The other stayed,
not moving away.

9.

Reggie told him
the full boorish story,

Of the rogue
who'd become gory.

"You want me,
to help you out?"

"Yes," said Reggie,
"But he carries a clout."

10.

"I know,
but he can't be allowed to win.

Justice is needed,
against his sin."

Reggie knew it to be true,
in his heart,

Confrontation was inevitable,
from the start.

11.

Both heard the rogue
trumpet from far away,

They headed toward the sound,
into the fray.

All eyes were on them,
elephant saw them too,

He knew what was coming,
and what to do.

12.

All three animals stopped close,
before standing still,

The situation was on,
each with looks that could kill.

"What do you want?"
elephant flapped his huge ears,

A terrifying sight,
he creating unimagined fears.

13.

Reggie said,
"We're here to reason with you,

Behaving badly
is not a sensible view.

Others respect
your need for a free life,

But you can't keep causing,
all this strife."

14.

"Strife is what you'll both get,
if I get irate,

I capable of taking on you,
and your mate!"

Reggie said,
"You're out of step, and time,

The way you've acted
has become a crime."

15.

"It's your last chance
to pass this social test,

But don't blow it,
do what's for the best.

The majorities had enough,
and you'll fail.

You'll age,
and younger animals will prevail."

16.

"You're big,
and can tackle either one,

But together we'll take you,
you'll be done.

The park is united,
that we win the day,

That's the last thing
I'm going to say."

17.

The Rhinos moved forward,
resolve of steel,

The stunned elephant,
the vultures next meal.

He stumbled,
it was all the rhino's would need,

Off of the elephant's fear,
they did feed.

18.

Reggie said,
"Let's settle this once and for all,

If you bully we'll attack,
and you will fall.

Back off gracefully,
allow others space.

This park's for us all,
it's everyone's place."

SUNBUDDY FABLES #6

19.

Elephant knew
he'd been over the top,

And in his heart,
knew it had to stop.

Majority opinion
couldn't be ignored,

The rogue was pacified,
peace was restored.

BERT THE (Water) BUFFALO

(London, UK) 26-09-1995

BERT THE WATER BUFFALO

1.

Bert the young buff
couldn't be told,

Making him
dangerously bold.

Danger didn't register,
in his brain

Feeling so invincible,
he'd never feel pain.

2.

Safe in the world,
confident and sure,

He just didn't know
the African score.

For animals there,
it's a dangerous attitude,

As lions or hyenas,
sustain their brood.

3.

Safety in numbers
is the best to hope for

With no guarantee,
from a slashing paw.

Lions hunt in a praid,
hyenas in a pack,

You never know next,
who will attack.

4.

Other tried to tell him,
of this danger,

He felt stronger,
than any predatory stranger.

He was reckless,
and at times blasé,

Being in danger,
in a wildlife play.

BERT THE WATER BUFFALO

5.

Lions observed,
he'd strayed from his herd,

Purring contentedly,
knowing he was absurd.

A young buff,
alone for them is a sitting duck,

Not believing they're good fortune,
and luck.

6.

Six lionesses ran at Bert,
not breaking stride,

A fearsome sight,
this lethal praid.

He instantly knew
he'd blown it big time,

For cats it was survival,
and no crime.

7.

He instinctly retreated,
it was all he do

Dust blew up,
smearing the sky blue.

The praid were not detered,
from their attack,

Running towards him,
never looking back.

8.

The other buffs were close,
all huge and black,

Hoping to reach them,
before the lions attack.

Two lionesses caught him,
each side they took,

Knowing they were there,
he didn't have to look.

BERT THE WATER BUFFALO

9.

Their overall weight was too much,
he was downed,

Losing his footing,
he crashed to the ground.

He got up and faced them,
he only thing left to do

Events unwinded rapidly,
lionesses arrived two by two.

10.

There was six now.
the end would be soon

He hadn't acted like a buffalo,
but a buffoon!

Lesson learnt,
but it was far too late,

He would perish,
by a horrible fate.

11.

Then other buffs charged,
changing his plight,

Surrounded him,
which was a wonderful sight.

The outnumbered lions,
beat a hasty retreat

The praid had to go elsewhere
for fresh meat.

12.

Growling angrily,
as their case was forlorn,

It was his biggest day
since he was born.

He thought,
"I don't believe I'm still here,"

His legs shook,
as he tried to control his fear.

13.

The furious buffs turned towards him,
and rightly so,

He cowered in front,
receiving their verbal blow.

"What have you learnt,"
the elder asked the calf,

"And answer with humility,
this is no laugh."

14.

"Always stay within the herd,
don't stray away,

Because you're open to attack,
from any prey."

"What else," said elder,
"What's as important as that?

Or you'll get eaten,
by a hyena or a cat."

15.

"I've got to listen,"
Bert said in reply,

The tension evaporated,
all did moo and sigh.

"Exactly," said the elder,
"Grasp the information.

Or days like today,
are your final destination."

16.

"Knowledge is special,
no creature knows it all.

Whether a wise owl,
or a giraffe so tall.

Pass this on to others,
when it's your turn,

To survive,
all buffalo have to listen and learn."

THE END